Rowan Blanchard

Star of Girl Meets World

by Lucas Diver

ABDO
POP BIOS
Kids

abdopublishing.com

Published by Abdo Kids, a division of ABDO, PO Box 398166, Minneapolis, Minnesota 55439.

Copyright © 2015 by Abdo Consulting Group, Inc. International copyrights reserved in all countries. No part of this book may be reproduced in any form without written permission from the publisher.

Printed in the United States of America, North Mankato, Minnesota.

102014

012015

 THIS BOOK CONTAINS RECYCLED MATERIALS

Photo Credits: AP Images, iStock, © Helga Esteb p.5, 9, 21, © s_buckley p.7, 11 / Shutterstock.com

Production Contributors: Teddy Borth, Jennie Forsberg, Grace Hansen

Design Contributors: Laura Rask, Dorothy Toth

Library of Congress Control Number: 2014943787

Cataloging-in-Publication Data

Diver, Lucas.

 Rowan Blanchard: star of Girl Meets World / Lucas Diver.

  p. cm. -- (Pop bios)

Includes index.

ISBN 978-1-62970-728-0

1. Blanchard, Rowan, 2001- --Juvenile literature. 2. Actors --United States--Biography--Juvenile literature. 1. Title.

791.4302--dc23

[B]

2014943787

Table of Contents

Early Life

Rowan Blanchard was born on October 14, 2001. She was born in Los Angeles, California.

Rowan loved to **perform** from a young age. Her parents would have friends over. Rowan would put on shows for them.

Rowan started acting at age five. Her first paid part was in a **commercial**. It was for **Apple**.

Spy Kids 4

In 2011, Rowan got a part in *Spy Kids 4*. She played Rebecca Wilson.

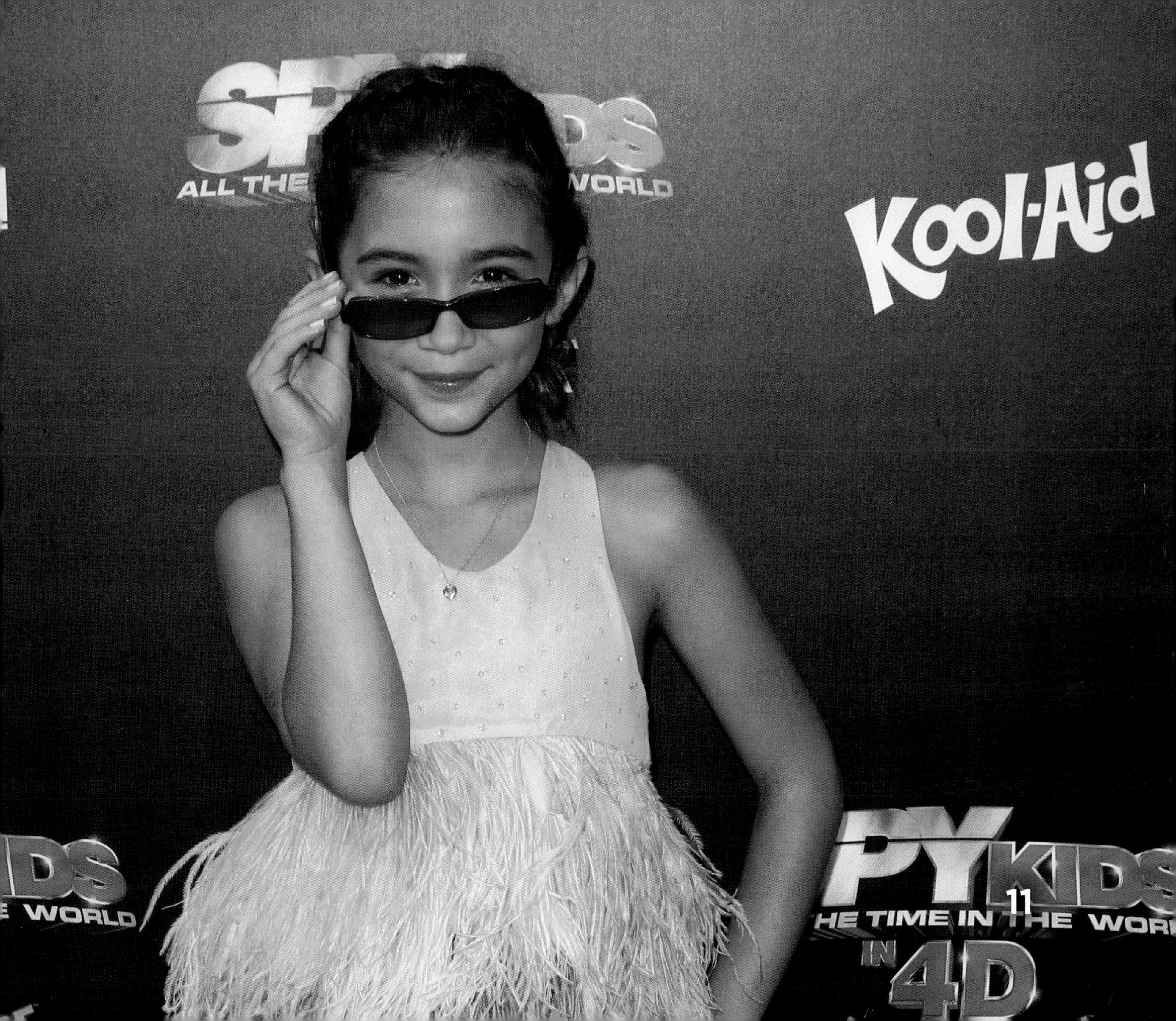
Kool-Aid
IN
4D

Girl Meets World

In 2013, Disney **announced** a new show. It was called *Girl Meets World*. Rowan would play Riley Matthews.

Riley is in seventh grade. She is happy and **responsible**. She is a good student. Rowan says she is like Riley in many ways.

15

Riley is the daughter of

Cory and Topanga Matthews.

They were characters in

Boy Meets World.

17

In 2014, Rowan got good news.

Girl Meets World was renewed

for a second season.

19

Stay Tuned!

Rowan has starred in movies
and on TV. At such a young
age, she has a lot more to give!

21

Timeline

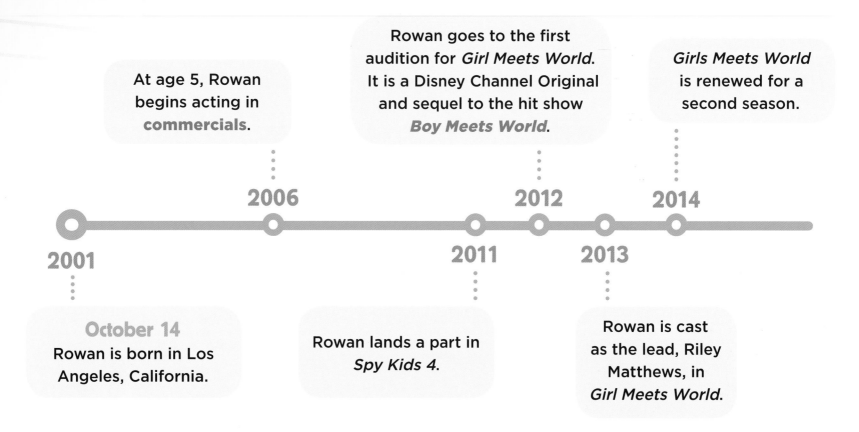

At age 5, Rowan begins acting in **commercials**.

Rowan goes to the first audition for *Girl Meets World*. It is a Disney Channel Original and sequel to the hit show *Boy Meets World*.

Girls Meets World is renewed for a second season.

2006

2012

2014

2001

2011

2013

October 14
Rowan is born in Los Angeles, California.

Rowan lands a part in *Spy Kids 4*.

Rowan is cast as the lead, Riley Matthews, in *Girl Meets World*.

Glossary

announce – to make something known to the public.

Apple – a company that designs, creates, and sells personal computers, tablets, and more.

Boy Meets World – a television show on ABC from 1993 to 2000.

commercial – a television or radio advertisement. An advertisement promotes a product, event, or service.

perform – to entertain an audience by singing, acting, etc.

responsible – able to be trusted to do what is right.

23

Index

abdokids.com

Use this code to log on to abdokids.com and access crafts, games, videos, and more!

Abdo Kids Code:
PRK7280